Penguin Education
Junior Voices The second book
edited by Geoffrey Summerfield

Junior Voices The second book

Junior Voices The first book
Junior Voices The third book
Junior Voices The fourth book
Junior Voices Teachers' handbook

edited by Geoffrey Summerfield

With 31 illustrations, 13 in colour

Penguin Books

Penguin Books Ltd, Harmondsworth,
Middlesex, England
Penguin Books Australia Ltd, Ringwood,
Victoria, Australia

First published 1970
This selection copyright © Geoffrey Summerfield, 1970

Filmset in Great Britain by
Butler & Tanner Ltd, Frome and London
Colour reproduction by Newgate Press Ltd,
London
Made and printed by W. S. Cowell Ltd,
at the Butter Market, Ipswich

Contents

Traditional English Riddles   1
Anonymous Who Said?   2
Kenneth Patchen The Little Man with Wooden Hair   2
Dylan Thomas A Conversation   5
Vachel Lindsay The Mouse that Gnawed the Oak-Tree Down   6
William Carlos Williams To be Closely Written on a Small Piece of Paper which Folded into a Tight Lozenge Will Fit Any Girl's Locket   6
Anthony Barton The Tramp Tree   8
Traditional American One Bright Morning   8
Traditional North American Indian Dream Song   10
May Swenson The Cloud-Mobile   10
James Kirkup In a Sailplane   13
A. R. Ammons Sitting Down, Looking Up   15
Traditional Australian Aboriginal Song: The Railway Train   15
William Carlos Williams Between Walls   15
Mei-Lan Law Roads   17
Buson Borrowed Armour   17
Onitsura The World Upside Down   17
Bashō Sudden Shower   17
Traditional American Didn't It Rain   20
Traditional American It ain't gonna rain no more, no more   20
Traditional Siberian Praise Song of the Wind   21
Traditional Marshall Islands Storm Tide on Mejit   24
Lou Lipsitz Over the dark highway   25
Gary Lewis The Computer's Spring Greeting   25
Shiki Summer Night   26
David Hill Dull Day   26
W. B. Yeats The Cat and the Moon   28
Ted Hughes Tree-Disease   29
Walter de la Mare Which?   29
Traditional Irish Slieve Gua   31

Carl Sandburg I am John Jones   31
Mary Neville Social Studies   31
Gwendolyn Brooks Nora   32
Susan David Poem   32
Patricia Hubbell Gravel Paths   32
John Donald Williams Angry   33
Carl Sandburg What's the matter up there?   33
Traditional American The Big Rock Candy Mountains   36
William Makepeace Thackeray A Tragic Story   38
Traditional American The Signifying Monkey   39
Traditional English Ooh!   42
Kenneth Patchen Day of Rabblement   42
Eve Merriam Mean Song   43
Traditional English The Feast of Lanterns   43
Traditional English We four lads from Liverpool are   43
Traditional American Rattlesnake   44
Robin Skelton Riches   45
Charles Reznikoff On a Sunday   45
Charles Reznikoff The shopgirls leave their work   45
Kikaku The cock again   46
Onitsura The Open-Air Bath   46
Peter Kelso The Bee   46
Buson The Whale   46
J. R. R. Tolkien *from* Oliphaunt   49
Anonymous Beg Parding   49
May Swenson Cat and the Weather   50
Vasko Popa Duck   51
May Swenson Feel Like a Bird   52
James Earp The Rook   53
Traditional Eskimo Eskimo Hunting Song   54
Melvin Walker la Follette The Ballad of Red Fox   55
May Swenson Living Tenderly   57
Traditional Scottish Earwig   57
Traditional Eskimo Two Paddler's Songs   59
Robert Graves The Six Badgers   59
Kenneth Patchen The Magical Mouse   61
Traditional English Four Charms   64
Traditional English Transmogrifications   65
Traditional American The Hairy Toe   65
Christian Morgenstern The Knee   67
Christian Morgenstern The Two Roots   67

Mark van Doren Dunce Song 68

William Carlos Williams The Thinker 69

Eleanor Farjeon Meeting Mary 71

Eve Merriam Teevee 72

F. Scott Fitzgerald In the fall of '16 72

Alastair Reid Words 74

Theodore Roethke The Chair 78

Theodore Roethke The Ceiling 79

Christian Morgenstern The Sniffle 79

James Payn I never had a piece of toast 79

Charles Reznikoff The Indian of Peru, I think 80

Answers to Riddles 82

Acknowledgements 83

List of Illustrations 85

Index of Titles and First Lines 86

Index of Poets, Translators and Collectors 88

Riddles

It is in the rock, but not in the stone;
It is in the marrow, but not in the bone;
It is in the bolster, but not in the bed;
It is not in the living, nor yet in the dead.

The land was white,
  The seed was black;
It'll take a good scholar
  To riddle me that.

On yonder hill there is a red deer,
The more you shoot it, the more you may,
You cannot drive that deer away.

As I went over London Bridge
Upon a cloudy day
I met a fellow clothed in yellow.
I took him up and sucked his blood,
And threw his skin away.

In marble halls as white as milk,
Lined with a skin as soft as silk,
Within a fountain crystal-clear,
A golden apple doth appear.
No doors there are to this stronghold,
Yet thieves break in and steal the gold.

TRADITIONAL ENGLISH

Who Said?

'There's-not-a cobbler-in-the-world-
Can-make-a shoe-to-me-
To-me-to-me-to-me-
Why-so-why-so-why-so-why-so?-
Because-my-heel's-as-long-as-my-toe-
My-toe-my-toe-my-toe!'

ANONYMOUS

The Little Man with Wooden Hair

There was a little man with wooden hair
Who'd sneak into the rear of buses
And holler, 'Somebody just ate my mother!'
For that way, of course, he could count on a quick trim
Without having to pay for the broken window.

KENNETH PATCHEN

A Conversation

ROSIE PROBERT   What seas did you see,
Tom Cat, Tom Cat,
In your sailoring days
Long long ago?
What sea beasts were
In the wavery green
When you were my master?

CAPTAIN CAT   I'll tell you the truth.
Seas barking like seals,
Blue seas and green,
Seas covered with eels
And mermen and whales.

ROSIE   What seas did you sail
Old whaler when
On the blubbery waves
Between Frisco and Wales
You were my bosun?

CAPTAIN CAT   As true as I'm here
You landlubber Rosie
You cosy love
My easy as easy
My true sweetheart,
Seas green as a bean
Seas gliding with swans
In the seal-barking moon.

DYLAN THOMAS

The Mouse that Gnawed the Oak-Tree Down

The mouse that gnawed the oak-tree down
Began his task in early life.
He kept so busy with his teeth
He had no time to take a wife.

He gnawed and gnawed through sun and rain
When the ambitious fit was on,
Then rested in the sawdust till
A month of idleness had gone.

He did not move about to hunt
The coteries of mousie-men.
He was a snail-paced, stupid thing
Until he cared to gnaw again.

The mouse that gnawed the oak-tree down,
When that tough foe was at his feet –
Found in the stump no angel-cake
Nor buttered bread, nor cheese nor meat –

The forest-roof let in the sky.
'This light is worth the work,' said he.
'I'll make this ancient swamp more light,'
And started on another tree.

VACHEL LINDSAY

To Be Closely Written on a Small Piece of Paper Which Folded into a Tight Lozenge Will Fit Any Girl's Locket

Lo the leaves
Upon the new autumn grass –
Look at them well. !

WILLIAM CARLOS WILLIAMS

The Tramp Tree

The tree with braces angin out
Like rags of a Tramp.
When the tree sways in the wind
Its like a tramps arm with hairs on.
Their fingers at the top of the tree,
Their tearing fingers,
Tearing holes in the sky,
Trying to grab what isn't there
Trying to get free.
Spiky grass is his hair
And half his head is under the grass
With his brain as dirt
The roots are like veins
Pulled out with the strength of his arms
His body with worms all wriggling about
Keeping him down
The stones that he eats
Fall down his throat
And stop at an end.

ANTHONY BARTON Age 9

One Bright Morning

One bright morning in the middle of the night,
Two dumb boys got up to fight.
Back to back they faced each other,
Drew their swords and shot each other.
A deaf policeman heard the noise,
Came and arrested those two dumb boys.

TRADITIONAL AMERICAN

Dream Song

Daybreak people have been chirping.
Above on the roof
Alighting they chirp.

TRADITIONAL
North American Indian poem translated from the Wintu by D. Demetracopoulou

The Cloud-Mobile

Above my face is a map
where continents form and fade.
Blue countries, made
on a white sea, are erased;
white countries are traced
on a blue sea.

It is a map that moves
faster than real
but so slow;
only my watching proves
that island has being,
or that bay.

It is a model of time;
mountains are wearing away,
coasts cracking, the ocean
spills over, then new
hills heap into view
with river-cuts of blue between them.

It is a map of change:
this is the way things are
with a stone or a star.
This is the way things go,
hard or soft,
swift or slow.

MAY SWENSON

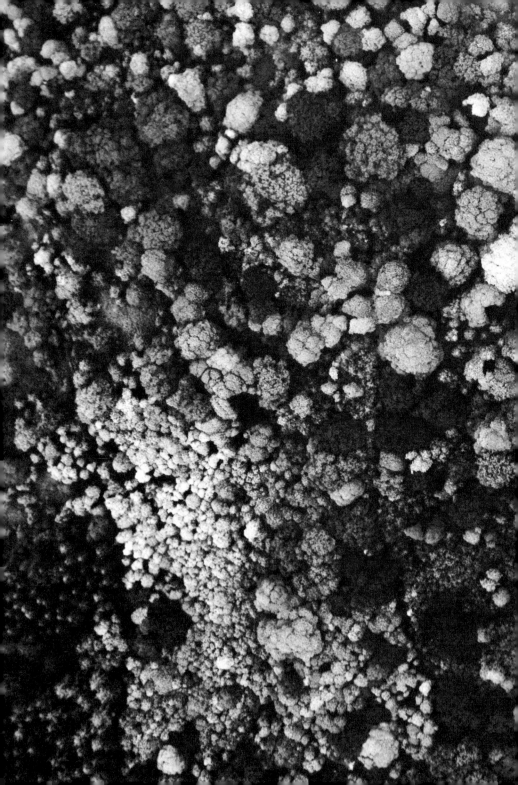

In a Sailplane

Still as a bird
Transfixed in flight
We shiver and flow
Into leagues of light.

Rising and turning
Without a sound
As summer lifts us
Off the ground.

The sky's deep bell
Of glass rings down.
We slip in a sea
That cannot drown.

We kick the wide
Horizon's blues
Like a cluttering hoop
From round our shoes.

This easy plane
So quietly speaks,
Like a tree it sighs
In silvery shrieks.

Neatly we soar
Through a roaring cloud:
Its caverns of snow
Are dark and loud.

Into banks of sun
Above the drifts
Of quilted cloud
Our stillness shifts.

Here no curious
Bird comes near.
We float alone
In a snowman's sphere.

Higher than spires
Where breath is rare
We beat the shires
Of racing air.

Up the cliff
Of sheer no-place
We swarm a rope
That swings on space.

Breezed by a star's
Long-drawn-out Protracted stare
We watch the earth
Drop out of air.

Red stars of light
Burn on the round
Of land: street-constellations
Strew the ground.

Their bridges leap
From town to town:
Into lighted dusk
We circle down.

Still as a bird
Transfixed in flight
We come to nest
In the field of night.

JAMES KIRKUP

Sitting Down, Looking Up

A silver jet,
riding the top of tundra clouds,
comes over
maybe from Rio:
the aluminium sun shines
on it
as if it were a natural creature.

A. R. AMMONS

Song: The Railway Train

You see the smoke at Kapunda
The steam puffs regularly,
Showing quickly, it looks like frost,
It runs like running water,
It blows like a spouting whale.

TRADITIONAL Australian Aboriginal poem translated by George Taplin

Between Walls

the back wings
of the

hospital where
nothing

will grow lie
cinders

in which shine
the broken

pieces of a green
bottle

WILLIAM CARLOS WILLIAMS

16 een bumfrey

Roads

Twisting turning
clinging to the contours of the earth
black – black as night
with white lines down its back.

MEI-LAN LAW Age 11

Borrowed Armour

Borrowed armour, old,
   getting fitted to my body –
      oh, it's cold!

BUSON Japanese poem translated by Harold G. Henderson

The World Upside Down

A trout leaps high –
   below him, in the river bottom,
      clouds flow by.

ONITSURA Japanese poem translated by Harold G. Henderson

Sudden Shower

Not even a hat –
   and cold rain falling on me?
      Tut-tut! think of that!

BASHŌ Japanese poem translated by Harold G. Henderson

18 tother bumfrey

Didn't It Rain

Now, didn't it rain, chillun,
God's gonna 'stroy this world with water,
Now didn't it rain, my Lord,
Now didn't it rain, rain, rain.

Well, it rained forty days and it rained forty nights,
There wasn't no land nowhere in sight,
God sent a raven to carry the news,
He histe his wings and away he flew.

lifted, hoisted

Well, it rained forty days and forty nights without
    stopping,
Noah was glad when the rain stopped a-dropping.
God sent Noah a rainbow sign,
Says, 'No more water, but fire next time.'

They knocked at the window and they knocked at the
    door,
They cried, 'O Noah, please take me on board.'
Noah cried, 'You're full of sin,
The Lord's got the key and you can't get in.'

TRADITIONAL AMERICAN

It ain't gonna rain no more, no more

It ain't gonna rain no more, no more,
It ain't gonna rain no more;
How in the heck can I wash my neck
If it ain't gonna rain no more?

TRADITIONAL AMERICAN

Praise Song of the Wind

Trees with weak roots
I will strike, I the wind.
I will roar, I will whistle.

Haycocks built today
I will scatter, I the wind.
I will roar, I will whistle.

Badly made haycocks
I will carry off, I the wind.
I will roar, I will whistle.

Uncovered stacks of sheaves
I will soak through, I the wind.
I will roar, I will whistle.

Houses not tightly roofed
I will destroy, I the wind.
I will roar, I will whistle.

Hay piled in sheds
I will tear apart, I the wind.
I will roar, I will whistle.

Fire kindled in the road
I will set flickering, I the wind.
I will roar, I will whistle.

Houses with bad smoke-holes
I will shake, I the wind.
I will roar, I will whistle.

The farmer who does not think
I will make to think, I the wind.
I will roar, I will whistle.

The worthless slug-a-bed
I will wake, I the wind.
I will roar, I will whistle.

TRADITIONAL Siberian poem translated by W. Radloff and Willard R. Trask

Storm Tide on Mejit

The wind's spine is broken,
It blows less,
We perform the wind-tabu.
It grows still, still, still,
Wholly still,
The calm, the calm.
The wind-tabu, *e*,
Makes calm, calm, calm.
The surf, surf, surf,
The surf, surf, surf,
The surf, surf, surf,
Plunges, roars,
Plunges, roars,
Plunges, roars,
It flows up,
The sea covers the beach with foam,
It is full of the finest sand,
Stirring up the ground, stirring up the ground.
It slaps, slaps, slaps,
Slaps, slaps, slaps
On the beach, and roars.

TRADITIONAL
Marshall Islands poem translated from a Micronesian language
by Augustin Krämer and Willard R. Trask

Over the dark highway

Over the dark highway
over the woods
and the clusters of small houses,
the clouds appear

The great clouds of a winter twilight!

> When I see them I feel like a hundred men
> who know they have slipped out of prison
> without a trace

LOU LIPSITZ

The Computer's Spring Greeting

Spring gling
flingle jingle
jing wring
sing wing
bring ting
ring ding
dingle ding
ding a ling
ling a ring
ring ring
jing a ring
wing a ling
spring a ling
spring swing
wing ing
fling spring
sprang spring
SPR . . . . . . ING!
    SPRING

GARY LEWIS Age 9

Summer Night

A lightning flash:
   between the forest trees
     I have seen water.

SHIKI Japanese poem translated by Harold G. Henderson

Dull Day

The day was dull,
The smell of the air
was icy.

The colour of the air
was as Dark
as a wolf's coat,
Misty.

DAVID HILL Age 8

The Cat and the Moon

The cat went here and there
And the moon spun round like a top,
And the nearest kin of the moon,
The creeping cat, looked up.
Black Minnaloushe stared at the moon,
For, wander and wail as he would,
The pure cold light in the sky
Troubled his animal blood.
Minnaloushe runs in the grass
Lifting his delicate feet.
Do you dance, Minnaloushe, do you dance?
When two close kindred meet,
What better than call a dance?
Maybe the moon may learn,
Tired of that courtly fashion,
A new dance turn.
Minnaloushe creeps through the grass
From moonlit place to place,
The sacred moon overhead
Has taken a new phase.
Does Minnaloushe know that his pupils
Will pass from change to change,
And that from round to crescent,
From crescent to round they range?
Minnaloushe creeps through the grass
Alone, important and wise,
And lifts to the changing moon
His changing eyes.

W. B. YEATS

Tree-Disease

On the moon with great ease
You can catch tree-disease.
The symptoms are birds
Seeming interested in your words
And examining your ears.
Then a root peers
From under the nail
Of your big toe, then
You'd better get cured quick
Or you'll be really sick.

TED HUGHES

Which?

'What did you say?'
'I? Nothing.' 'No? . . .
What was that sound?'
'When?'
'Then.'
'I do not know.'
'Whose eyes were those on us?'
'Where?'
'There.'
'No eyes I saw.'
'Speech, footfall, presence – how cold the night may be!'
'Phantom or fantasy, it's all one to *me.*'

WALTER DE LA MARE

Slieve Gua

Gua Mountain

Slieve Gua, craggy and black wolf-den:
In the clefts the wind howls,
In its dens the wolves wail.

Autumn on Slieve Gua and the angry
bellows Brown deer bells, and herons
Croak across Slieve Gua's crags.

TRADITIONAL IRISH

I am John Jones

'I am John Jones.'
'Take a chair.'
'Yes, and I am the son of John
  Throckmorton Jones.'
'Is that possible? Take two chairs.'

CARL SANDBURG

Social Studies

Woody says, 'Let's *make* our soap.
It's easy.
We learned about it
In school.'
He told Mother,
'All you do is
Take a barrel.
Bore holes in the sides,
And fill it with straw.
Ashes on top – '

'No,' said Mother.

MARY NEVILLE

Nora

I was not sleeping when Brother said
'Good-bye!' and laughed and teased my head;
And went, like rockets, out of the door,
As he had done most days before.

But it was fun to curl between
The white warm sheets, and not be seen,

And stay, a minute more, alone,
Keeping myself for my very own.

GWENDOLYN BROOKS

Poem

I can hear the trees whispering
The cat purring
The dogs barking
no wonder I cant get to sleep
I can hear my dad in a rage
tearing up a page
into little bits
while my mother sits
crying
no wonder I cant get to sleep

SUSAN DAVID Age 8

Gravel Paths

I feel crinkled when I walk on gravel paths.
The gravel crinkles me
And I become gravel,
Crunched under five thousand footsteps.
I know what it is to be gravel,
Pecked at by pigeons,
Searching for crumbs of park picnics.

Gravel gets tired,
Being poked at by sparrows and pigeons,
Being squashed under grown-up feet,
Being combed by park men's tickling rakes.
Gravel would rather play,
plimsolls Explode in skittery sprays under running sneakers.
At least I think it would,
And I should know,
Having run crinkled
And sneaker-shod
Up many gravel paths.

PATRICIA HUBBELL

Angry

You feel as if you could jump on them,
As if to kill them in anger,
It feels as if you had the strength,
Of a hundred men.
You get in a kind of a trance,
And go pushing people about,
The slightest thing that goes wrong,
Makes you blame it on someone else.
If a person gets angry with you,
You try not to listen.

JOHN DONALD WILLIAMS Age 11

What's the matter up there?

'What's the matter up there?'
'Playing soldiers.'
'But soldiers don't make that kind of noise.'
'We're playing the kind of soldier that
makes that kind of noise.'

CARL SANDBURG

The Big Rock Candy Mountains

On a summer's day in the month of May,
tramp   A burly bum come a-hiking,
Travelling down that lonesome road
A-looking for his liking.
He was headed for a land that was far away,
Beside them crystal fountains –
autumn   'I'll see you all this coming fall
In the Big Rock Candy Mountains.'

In the Big Rock Candy Mountains
You never change your socks,
And little streams of alcohol
Come a-trickling down the rocks.
railway trucks   The box cars are all empty
policemen   And the railroad bulls are blind,
There's a lake of stew and whisky, too,
You can paddle all around 'em in a big canoe
In the Big Rock Candy Mountains.

O – the buzzing of the bees in the cigarette trees
Round the soda-water fountains,
Where the lemonade springs and the bluebird sings
In the Big Rock Candy Mountains.

In the Big Rock Candy Mountains,
There's a land that's fair and bright,
Where the hand-outs grow on bushes
And you sleep out every night,
Where the box cars are all empty
And the sun shines every day,
O I'm bound to go, where there ain't no snow,
Where the rain don't fall and the wind don't blow
In the Big Rock Candy Mountains.

In the Big Rock Candy Mountains
The jails are made of tin
And you can bust right out again
As soon as they put you in;
The farmers' trees are full of fruit,
The barns are full of hay,
I'm going to stay where you sleep all day,
Where they boiled in oil the inventor of toil
In the Big Rock Candy Mountains.

TRADITIONAL AMERICAN

A Tragic Story

wise man

There liv'd a sage in days of yore,
And he a handsome pigtail wore,
But wonder'd much and sorrow'd more,
Because it hung behind him.

He mus'd upon this curious case,
And swore he'd change the pigtail's place,
And have it hanging at his face,
Not dangling there behind him.

Says he, 'The mystery I've found –
I'll turn me round.'
He turn'd him round,
But still it hung behind him.

Then round and round, and out and in,
All day the puzzled sage did spin;
In vain – it matter'd not a pin,
The pigtail hung behind him.

And right and left, and round about,
And up and down, and in and out
He turn'd, but still the pigtail stout
Hung steadily behind him.

And though his efforts never slack,
And though he twist, and twirl, and tack,
Alas! still faithful to his back,
The pigtail hangs behind him.

WILLIAM MAKEPEACE THACKERAY

The Signifying Monkey

The Monkey and the Lion
Got to talking one day.
Monkey looked down and said, 'Lion,
I hear you're king in every way.
But I know somebody
Who do not think that is true –
He told me he could whip
The living daylights out of you.'
Lion said, 'Who?'
Monkey said, 'Lion,
He talked about your mama
And talked about your grandma, too,
And I'm too polite to tell you
What he said about you.'
Lion said, 'Who said what? Who?'
Monkey in the tree,
Lion on the ground.
Monkey kept on signifying
But he didn't come down.
Monkey said, 'His name is Elephant –
He stone sure is not your friend.'
Lion said, 'He don't need to be
Because today will be his end.'

Lion took off through the jungle
Lickity-split,
Meaning to grab Elephant
And tear him bit to bit. Full stop!
He came across Elephant copping a righteous nod
Under a fine cool shady tree.
Lion said, 'You big old no-good so-and-so,
It's either you or me.'
Lion let out a solid roar
And bopped Elephant with his paw.
Elephant just took his trunk
And busted old Lion's jaw.
Lion let out another roar,
Reared up six feet tall.
Elephant just kicked him in the belly
And laughed to see him drop and fall.
Lion rolled over,
Copped Elephant by the throat.
Elephant just shook him loose
And butted him like a goat,
Then he tromped him and he stomped him
Till the Lion yelled, 'Oh, no!'
And it was near-nigh sunset
When Elephant let Lion go.
The signifying Monkey
Was still sitting in his tree
When he looked down and saw the Lion.
Said, 'Why, Lion, who can that there be?'
Lion said, 'Monkey, I don't want
To hear your jive-end jive.'
Monkey just kept on signifying,
'Lion, you for sure caught hell –
Mister Elephant's whipped you
To a fare-thee-well!
You ain't no king to me.
Fact is, I don't think that you
Can even as much as roar –
And if you try I'm liable

To come down out of this tree and
Whip your tail some more.'
The Monkey started laughing
And jumping up and down.
But he jumped so hard the limb broke
And he landed – bam! – on the ground.
When he went to run, his foot slipped
And he fell flat down.
Grrr-rrr-rr-r! The Lion was on him
With his front feet and his hind.
Monkey hollered, 'Ow!
I didn't mean it, Mister Lion!'
Lion said, 'You little flea-bag you!
Why, I'll eat you up alive.
I wouldn't a-been in this fix a-tall
Wasn't for your signifying jive.'
'*Please*,' said Monkey, 'Mister Lion,
If you'll just let me go,
I got something to tell you, please,
I think you ought to know.'
Lion let the Monkey loose
To see what his tale could be –
And Monkey jumped right back on up
Into his tree.
'What I was gonna tell you,' said Monkey,
'Is you square old so-and-so,
If you fool with me I'll get
Elephant to whip your head some more.'
'Monkey,' said the Lion,
Beat to his unbooted knees,
'You and all your signifying children
Better stay up in them trees.'
Which is why today
Monkey does his signifying
A-way-up out of the way.

TRADITIONAL AMERICAN

Ooh!

Now, miller, miller, dustipole,
I'll clapper-claw your jobbernole!

TRADITIONAL ENGLISH

Day of Rabblement

O come here! a sunflower!
No no no no
O hurry! hurry!
A sunflower is standing here!

No no no no

O come here!
There's a sunflower beside the wall!
No no no no
Great God! hurry! a sunflower!

No no no no

A sunflower!
Come! look at the sunflower!
Sunflower!
No no no no
Then tell me why you
Won't come!
No no no no

No no no no.

KENNETH PATCHEN

Mean Song

Snickles and podes,
Ribble and grodes:
That's what I wish you.

A nox in the groot,
A root in the stoot
And a gock in the forbeshaw, too.

Keep out of sight
For fear that I might
Glom you a gravely snave.

Don't show your face
Around any place
Or you'll get one flack snack in the bave.

EVE MERRIAM

The Feast of Lanterns

Tching-a-ring-a-ring-tching,
Feast of Lanterns,
What a lot of chop-sticks, bombs and gongs;
Four-and-twenty thousand crink-um-crank-ums,
All among the bells and the ding-dongs.

TRADITIONAL ENGLISH

We four lads from Liverpool are

We four lads from Liverpool are:
Paul in a taxi, John in a car,
George on a scooter, tootin' his hooter,
Following Ringo Starr!

TRADITIONAL ENGLISH

Rattlesnake

Rattlesnake, O rattlesnake,
What makes your teeth so white?
I've been in the bottom all my life,
An' I ain't done nothin' but bite, bite,
Ain't done nothin' but bite.

Muskrat, O muskrat,
What makes you smell so bad?
I've been in the bottom all of my life
Till I'm mortified in my head, head,
I'm mortified in my head.

Groundhog, groundhog,
What makes your back so brown?
It's a wonder I don't smotherfy,
Livin' down in the ground, ground,
Livin' down in the ground.

Rooster, O rooster,
What makes your claws so hard?
Been scratchin' this gravel all my days,
It's a wonder I ain't tired, tired,
It's a wonder I ain't tired.

Jaybird, O jaybird,
What makes you fly so high?
Been robbin' your cornpatch all my life,
It's a wonder I don't die, die,
It's a wonder I don't die.

TRADITIONAL AMERICAN

Riches

The ditch in Humber Lane
Was black with tadpoles, round
Black beads and whippy tails;
I knelt down at the side,
And filled my jar as black
As now I fill this page,
Glad of the gathered life
However many died.

ROBIN SKELTON

On a Sunday

On a Sunday, when the place was closed,
I saw a plump mouse among the cakes in the window:
dear ladies,
who crowd this expensive tea-room,
you must not think that you alone are blessed of God.

CHARLES REZNIKOFF

The shopgirls leave their work

The shopgirls leave their work
quietly.

Machines are still, tables and chairs
darken.

The silent rounds of mice and roaches begin.

CHARLES REZNIKOFF

The cock again

The cock again
  is fighting like a lion:
    see his mane!

KIKAKU Japanese poem translated by Harold G. Henderson

The Open-Air Bath

There is no place
  to throw the used bath water.
    Insect cries!

ONITSURA Japanese poem translated by Harold G. Henderson

The Bee

The bee is a merchant.
He trades among
flower planets.

PETER KELSO Age 12

The Whale

A whale!
  Down it goes, and more and more
    up goes its tail!

BUSON Japanese poem translated by Harold G. Henderson

from Oliphaunt

Grey as a mouse,
Big as a house,
Nose like a snake,
I make the earth shake,
As I tramp through the grass;
Trees crack as I pass.
With horns in my mouth
I walk in the South,
Flapping big ears.
Beyond count of the years
I stump round and round,
Never lie on the ground,
Not even to die.
Oliphaunt am I,
Biggest of all,
Huge, old and tall.
If ever you'd met me,
You wouldn't forget me.
If ever you do,
You won't think I'm true;
But Old Oliphaunt am I,
And I never lie.

J. R. R. TOLKIEN

Beg Parding

'Beg parding, Mrs Harding,
Is my kitting in your garding?'
'Yes she is, and all alone,
Chewing of a mutting bone.'

ANONYMOUS

Cat and the Weather

Cat takes a look at the weather.
Snow.
Puts a paw on the sill.
His perch is piled, is a pillow.

Shape of his pad appears.
Will it dig? No.
Not like sand.
Like his fur almost.

But licked, not liked.
Too cold.
Insects are flying, fainting down.
He'll try

to bat one against the pane.
They have no body and no buzz.
And now his feet are wet;
it's a puzzle.

Shakes each leg,
then shakes his skin
to get the white flies off.
Looks for his tail,

tells it to come on in
by the radiator.
World's turned queer
somehow. All white,

no smell. Well, here
inside it's still familiar.
He'll go to sleep until
it puts itself right.

MAY SWENSON

Duck

She waddles through the dust
In which no fish are smiling
Within her sides she carries
The restlessness of water

Clumsy
She waddles slowly
The reeds she's thinking of
She'll reach them anyway

Never
Never will she be able
To walk
As she was able
To plough the mirrors

VASKO POPA
Yugoslavian poem translated from the Serbo-Croatian by Anne Pennington

Feel Like a Bird

Feel like a   Bird
Understand
He has no   Hand

Instead a   Wing
Close-lapped
mysterious thing

In sleeveless coat
he halves the   Air
skipping there

like water-licked boat
Lands on   Star-Toes
Finger-beak in

feather-pocket
finds no   Coin
In neat head like   Seeds

in a quartered apple
eyes join
sniping at   Opposites

to stereoscope
the scene before
Close to floor   Giddy

no arms to fling
a third   Sail
spreads for calm

his tail
Hand better than a   Wing
to gather a   Heap

to count
to clasp a   Mate?
Or leap

lone-free on muffled
shoulders to span
a   Fate?

MAY SWENSON

The Rook

Black as night it cuts through the air,
Its wide wings spread,
Flap and wave.
Scavenger.
Soft of touch,
But as tough as leather.
Oily wings like cast-off rags,
The rook.
A ready beak to tear and rip,
Eyes like coals, cold and dark,
With hoarse cry
And stupid.

JAMES EARP Age 12

Eskimo Hunting Song

I wanted to use my weapon.
There was a big blubbery seal on the ice, even here.
I struck smartly with my harpoon,
And then I just pulled it up, the seal wandering from
    one breathing-hole to another.

I wanted to use my weapon.
There was a big antlered caribou on the land, even down
    there.
I shot my arrow swiftly,
Then I just knocked it down in this place, the caribou
    that wandered about the land.

I wanted to use my weapon.
There was a fish right in the lake, even here.
I struck it smartly with my fish-spear,
Then I just pulled it up, the fish that wandered about
    down here.

I wanted to use my weapon.
There was a big bearded seal, just at the river-mouth,
    even here.
I paddled my kayak hard,
Then I simply towed it ashore, just at the river-mouth.

TRADITIONAL Eskimo poem translated by Sir Maurice Bowra

The Ballad of Red Fox

Yellow sun yellow
Sun yellow sun,
When, oh, when
Will red fox run?

When the hollow horn shall sound,
When the hunter lifts his gun
And liberates the wicked hound,
Then, oh, then shall red fox run.

Yellow sun yellow
Sun yellow sun,
Where, oh, where
Will red fox run?

Through meadows hot as sulphur,
Through forests cool as clay,
Through hedges crisp as morning
And grasses limp as day.

Yellow sky yellow
Sky yellow sky,
How, oh, how
Will red fox die?

With a bullet in his belly,
A dagger in his eye,
And blood upon his red red brush
Shall red fox die.

MELVIN WALKER LA FOLLETTE

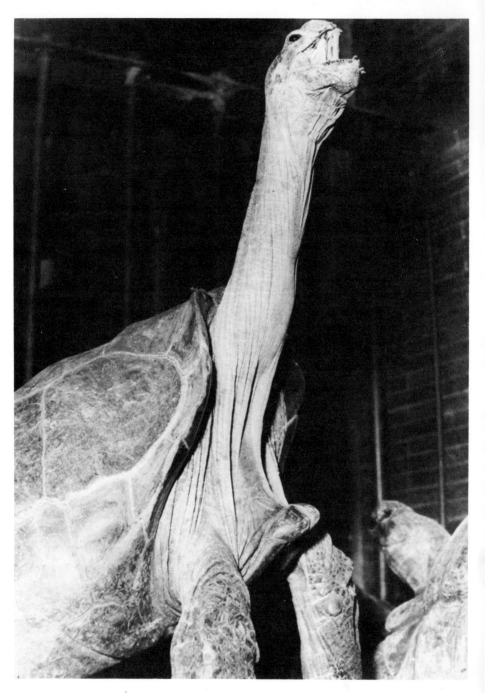

Living Tenderly

My body a rounded stone
with a pattern of smooth seams.
My head a short snake,
retractive, projective.
My legs come out of their sleeves
or shrink within,
and so does my chin.
My eyelids are quick clamps.

My back is my roof.
I am always at home.
I travel where my house walks.
It is a smooth stone.
It floats within the lake,
or rests in the dust.
My flesh lives tenderly
inside its bone.

MAY SWENSON

Earwig

The horny goloch is an awesome beast,
Supple and scaly;
It has two horns, and a hantle of feet,
And a forkie tailie.

TRADITIONAL SCOTTISH

Two Paddler's Songs

The Kayak Paddler's Joy at the Weather

When I'm out of the house in the open, I feel joy.
When I get out on the sea on hap-hazard, I feel joy.
If it is really fine weather, I feel joy.
If the sky really clears nicely, I feel joy.
May it continue thus for the good of my sealing!
May it continue thus for the good of my hunting!
May it continue thus for the good of my singing-match!
May it continue thus for the good of my drum-song!

Paddler's Song on Bad Hunting Weather

I got my poem in perfect order.
On the threshold of my tongue
Its arrangement was made.
But I failed, indeed, in my hunting.

TRADITIONAL Eskimo poems translated by William Thalbitzer

The Six Badgers

As I was a-hoeing, a-hoeing my lands
Six badgers came up with white wands in their hands.
They made a ring around me and, bowing, they said:
'Hurry home, Farmer George, for the table is spread!
There's pie in the oven, there's beef on the plate:
Hurry home, Farmer George, if you would not be late!'
So homeward I went, but could not understand
Why six fine dog-badgers with white wands in hand
Should seek me out hoeing and bow in a ring,
And all to inform me so common a thing!

ROBERT GRAVES

The Magical Mouse

I am the magical mouse
I don't eat cheese
I eat sunsets
And the tops of trees

I don't wear fur

I wear funnels
Of lost ships and the weather
That's under dead leaves
I am the magical mouse

I don't fear cats

Or woodowls
I do as I please
Always
I don't eat crusts
I am the magical mouse
I eat
Little birds and maidens

That taste like dust

KENNETH PATCHEN

Four Charms

Hey-how for Hallowe'en!
All the witches to be seen,
Some black, and some green,
Hey-how for Hallowe'en!

A Charm for Sprains

Baldur and Woden went to the wood.
There was Baldur's foal's foot sprained.
Then charmed Woden, as well he knew how
For bone sprain, for blood sprain, for limb sprain.
Bone to bone, blood to blood, limb to limbs
As though they were glued.

A Charm

Nail three horseshoes to the foot of the
patient's bed, with a hammer laid crosswise upon them,
and then strike them, with the hammer held in the left
hand, saying:

Father, Son and Holy Ghost,
Nail the devil to the post.
Thrice I strike with holy crook,
One for God and one for Wod and one for Lok.

A Charm for Burns

Breathe three times on the burnt place and say:

Here come I to cure a burnt sore.
If the dead knew what the living endure,
The burnt sore would burn no more.

TRADITIONAL ENGLISH

Transmogrifications

To change into a hare, say this:

I shall go into a hare
much With sorrow and sighing and mickle care,
And I shall go in the Devil's name
Till I come home again.

To change back to a human shape, say this:

Hare, hare, God send thee care.
I am in a hare's likeness now
But I shall be in a woman's likeness even now.

TRADITIONAL ENGLISH

The Hairy Toe

Once there was a woman went out to pick beans,
and she found a Hairy Toe.
She took the Hairy Toe home with her,
and that night, when she went to bed,
the wind began to moan and groan.
Away off in the distance
she seemed to hear a voice crying,
'Who's got my Hair-r-ry To-o-oe?
Who's got my Hair-r-ry To-o-oe?'

The woman scrooched down,
'way down under the covers,
and about that time
the wind appeared to hit the house,
smoosh,
and the old house creaked and cracked
like something was trying to get in.
The voice had come nearer,
almost at the door now,
and it said,

'Where's my Hair-r-ry To-o-oe?
Who's got my Hair-r-ry To-o-oe?'

The woman scrooched further down
under the covers
and pulled them tight around her head.
The wind growled around the house
like some big animal
and r-r-um-mbled
over the chimbley.
All at once she heard the door cr-r-a-ack
and Something slipped in
and began to creep over the floor.
The floor went
cre-e-eak, cre-e-eak
at every step that thing took towards her bed.
The woman could almost feel
it bending over her bed.
Then in an awful voice it said:
'Where's my Hair-r-ry To-o-oe?
Who's got my Hair-r-ry To-o-oe?
You've got it!'

TRADITIONAL AMERICAN

The Knee

On earth there roams a lonely knee.
It's just a knee, that's all.
It's not a tent, it's not a tree,
it's just a knee, that's all.

In battle, long ago, a man
was riddled through and through.
The knee alone escaped unhurt
as if it were taboo.

Since then there roams a lonely knee,
it's just a knee, that's all.
It's not a tent, it's not a tree,
it's just a knee, that's all.

CHRISTIAN MORGENSTERN German poem translated by Max Knight

The Two Roots

A pair of pine roots, old and dark,
make conversation in the park.

The whispers where the top leaves grow
are echoed in the roots below.

An agèd squirrel sitting there
is knitting stockings for the pair.

The one says: squeak. The other: squawk.
That is enough for one day's talk.

CHRISTIAN MORGENSTERN German poem translated by Max Knight

Dunce Song

If I had a wife
I would love her as kings
Loved queens in the old days, or as princes
Maidens,
Met in the dew, by a stile, of a morning –
'How do you do, my pretty?'
And all of that.

If I had a wife
I would come home sometimes
Dressed like a stranger, and when she stared,
'Lady,'
I'd say, and woo her in wonder –
'How can there be such shining?'
And all of that.

If I had a wife
I would never be done
With remembering how it is now when, oh,
I am lonesome,
And no one is here but my dog and my cat –
'Well, old boys! Hungry?'
And all of that.

MARK VAN DOREN

The Thinker

My wife's new pink slippers
have gay pom-poms.
There is not a spot or a stain
on their satin toes or their sides.
All night they lie together
under her bed's edge.
Shivering I catch sight of them
and smile, in the morning.
Later I watch them
descending the stair,
hurrying through the doors
and round the table,
moving stiffly
with a shake of their gay pom-poms!
And I talk to them
in my secret mind
out of pure happiness.

WILLIAM CARLOS WILLIAMS

Meeting Mary

Hard by the Wildbrooks I met Mary,
When berries smelled sweet and hot.
Mary, I fancy, was seven years old,
And I am never mind what.

'What are you getting?' I asked Mary.
'Blackberries. What are you?'
'Toadflax,' I answered Mary, 'and mushrooms.'
'How many mushrooms?' 'Two.'

'Going to have blackberries stewed for dinner,
  Or blackberry jam?' said I.
'Not goin' to have neither,' said Mary;
'Goin' to have blackberry pie.'

'Aren't you lucky!' I said to Mary.
'And what sort of name have you got?'
'*My* name's Mary,' said Mary, 'what's *your* name?'
I told her never mind what.

'Good-bye, Mary.' 'Good-bye,' said Mary,
And went on picking and eating.
That's all about my meeting with Mary –
It's my favourite sort of meeting.

ELEANOR FARJEON

Teevee

In the house
of Mr and Mrs Spouse
he and she
would watch teevee
and never a word
between them spoken
until the day
the set was broken.

Then 'How do you do?'
said he to she,
'I don't believe
that we've met yet.
Spouse is my name.
What's yours?' he asked.

'Why, mine's the same!'
said she to he,
'Do you suppose that we could be –?'

But the set came suddenly right about,
and so they never did find out.

EVE MERRIAM

In the fall of '16

autumn

In the fall of '16 in the cool of the afternoon
I met Caroline under a white moon
There was an orchestra – Bingo-Bango
Playing for us to dance the tango
And the people all clapped as we arose
For her sweet face and my new clothes –

F. SCOTT FITZGERALD

Words

Words To Be Said on the Move

FLIT
FLUCTUATE
WOBBLE
WIGGLE
SHIVER
TIPTOE
PIROUETTE
TWIRL
TEETER

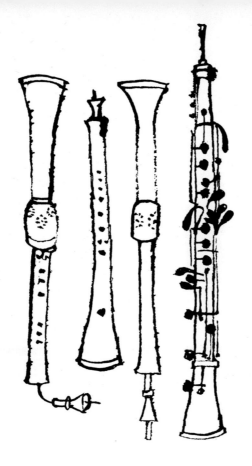

Odd Words

(to be spoken out loud, for fun)

HOBNOB
BARLEY
DOG-EARED
HOPSCOTCH
WINDWARD
OAF
EGG
OBOE
NUTMEG
OBLONG

Light Words

(to be said in windy or singing moods)

ARIEL
WILLOW
SPINNAKER
WHIRR
LISSOM
SIBILANT
PETTICOAT
NIMBLE
NIB

Heavy Words

(to be used in gloom or bad weather)

DUFFLE
BLUNDERBUSS
GALOSHES
BOWL
BEFUDDLED
MUGWUMP
PUMPKIN
CRUMB
BLOB

ALASTAIR REID

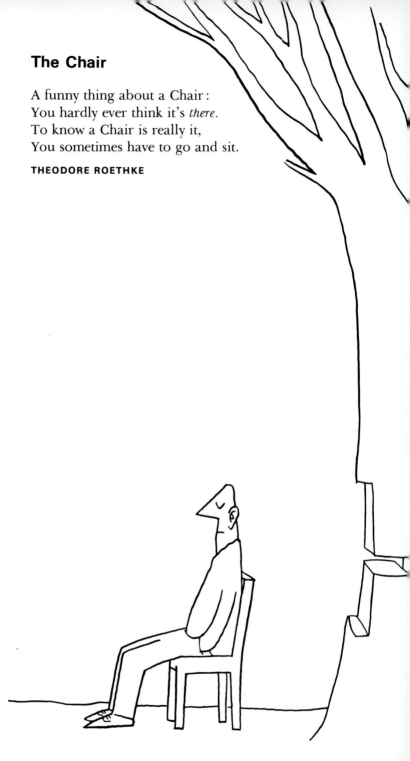

The Chair

A funny thing about a Chair:
You hardly ever think it's *there*.
To know a Chair is really it,
You sometimes have to go and sit.

THEODORE ROETHKE

The Ceiling

Suppose the Ceiling went Outside
And then caught Cold and Up and Died?
The only Thing we'd have for Proof
That he was Gone, would be the Roof;
I think it would be Most Revealing
To find out how the Ceiling's Feeling.

THEODORE ROETHKE

The Sniffle

A sniffle crouches on the terrace
to catch a victim he could harass.

And suddenly he jumps with vim
upon a man by name of Schrimm.

Paul Schrimm, responding with 'hatchoo',
is stuck with him the weekend through.

CHRISTIAN MORGENSTERN German poem translated by Max Knight

I never had a piece of toast

I never had a piece of toast
Particularly long and wide,
But fell upon the sanded floor
And always on the buttered side.

JAMES PAYN

The Indian of Peru, I think

The Indian of Peru, I think,
chewing
the leaf of a shrub
could run all day.
I, too,
with a few lines of verse, only two or three,
may be able
to see the day through.

CHARLES REZNIKOFF

Answers to Riddles

Riddles page 1

1 The letter R   2 Print on a page   3 The rising sun
4 A blood orange   5 A hen's egg

Who Said? page 2

The Lark

Acknowledgements

For permission to use copyright material acknowledgement is made to the following:

Poetry   For 'Sitting Down, Looking Up' from *Northfield Poems* by A. R. Ammons to Cornell University Press; for 'The Tramp Tree' by Anthony Barton to the *Daily Mirror* Children's Literary Competition; for 'Sudden Shower' by Bashō from *An Introduction to Haiku* edited by Harold G. Henderson to Doubleday & Co. Inc.; for 'Eskimo Hunting Song' translated by Sir Maurice Bowra from *The Unwritten Song* edited by Willard R. Trask to the Macmillan Company of New York; for 'Nora' from *Bronzeville Boys and Girls* by Gwendolyn Brooks to Harper & Row Inc.; for 'Borrowed Armour' and 'The Whale' by Buson from *An Introduction to Haiku* edited by Harold G. Henderson to Doubleday & Co. Inc.; for 'Poem' by Susan David to the *Daily Mirror* Children's Literary Competition; for 'Dream Song' translated by D. Demetracopoulou from *The Unwritten Song* edited by Willard R. Trask to the Macmillan Company of New York; for 'The Rook' by James Earp to the *Daily Mirror* Children's Literary Competition; for 'Meeting Mary' from *Poems for Children* by Eleanor Farjeon to David Higham Associates Ltd and J. B. Lippincott Company; for 'In the fall of '16' from *Sleeping and Waking* by F. Scott Fitzgerald from Volume 3 of *The Bodley Head Scott Fitzgerald* to The Bodley Head and from *The Crack-Up* to New Directions Publishing Corporation; for 'The Ballad of Red Fox' by Melvin Walker la Follette from *The New Yorker, 1952* to the author; for 'The Six Badgers' from *The Penny Fiddle* by Robert Graves to the author and Collins-Knowlton-Wing Inc.; for 'Dull Day' by David Hill to the *Daily Mirror* Children's Literary Competition; for 'Gravel Paths' from *Catch Me a Wind* by Patricia Hubbell to Atheneum Publishers Inc.; for 'Tree-Disease' from *The Earth Owl and Other Moon People* by Ted Hughes to Faber & Faber Ltd; for 'The Bee' by Peter Kelso from *Once Around the Sun* to the Oxford University Press (Australia); for 'The Cock Again' by Kikaku from *An Introduction to Haiku* edited by Harold G. Henderson to Doubleday & Co. Inc.; for 'In a Sailplane' by James Kirkup to the author; for 'Storm Tide on Mejit' translated by Augustin Kramer and Willard R. Trask from *The Unwritten Song* edited by Willard R. Trask to the Macmillan Company of New York; for 'Roads' by Mei-Lan Law from *Once Around the Sun* to the Oxford University Press (Australia); for 'The Computer's Spring Greeting' by Gary Lewis to the author; for 'Over the Dark Highway' from *Cold Water* by Lou Lipsitz to Wesleyan University Press; for 'The Mouse that Gnawed the Oak-Tree down' from *Collected Poems* by Vachel Lindsay to the Macmillan Company of New York; for 'Which' by Walter de la Mare to the Literary Trustees of Walter de la Mare and the Society of Authors, for 'Mean Song' from *There is No Rhyme for Silver* by Eve Merriam to Atheneum Publishers Inc.; for 'Teevee' from *Catch a Little Rhyme* by Eve Merriam to the author and Atheneum Publishers Inc.; for 'The Knee', 'The Sniffle' and 'The Two Roots' from *Gallows Songs* by Christian Morgenstern translated by Max Knight to the University of California Press; for 'Social Studies' from *Woody and Me* by Mary Neville to McIntosh & Otis Inc. and Pantheon Books Inc.; for 'The Open-Air Bath' and 'The World Upside Down' by Onitsura from *An Introduction to Haiku* edited by Harold G. Henderson to Doubleday & Co. Inc.; for 'Day of Rabblement' from *When We Were Here Together* by Kenneth Patchen and for 'The Little Man with Wooden Hair' from

Hurrah for Anything by Kenneth Patchen to New Directions Publishing Corporation; for 'The Magical Mouse' from *Collected Poems* by Kenneth Patchen to Jonathan Cape Ltd and New Directions Publishing Corporation; for 'Duck' from *Selected Poems* by Vasko Popa translated by Anne Pennington to Olwyn Hughes; for 'Praise Song of the Wind' translated by W. Radloff and Willard R. Trask from *The Unwritten Song* edited by Willard R. Trask to the Macmillan Company of New York; for 'Words' from *Ounce, Dice, Trice* by Alastair Reid to J. M. Dent & Sons Ltd and Atlantic-Little, Brown & Co.; for 'The Indian of Peru', 'On a Sunday' and 'The shopgirls leave their work' from *By the Waters of Manhattan* by Charles Reznikoff to New Directions Publishing Corporation; for 'The Ceiling' and 'The Chair' from *Collected Poems* by Theodore Roethke to Faber & Faber Ltd and Doubleday & Co. Inc.; for 'I am John Jones' and 'What's the matter up there?' from *The People, Yes* by Carl Sandburg to Harcourt, Brace & World Inc.; for 'Summer Night' by Shiki from *An Introduction to Haiku* edited by Harold G. Henderson to Doubleday & Co. Inc.; for 'Riches' by Robin Skelton to McClelland & Stewart Ltd; for 'Cat and the Weather', 'The Cloud-Mobile', 'Feel Like a Bird' and 'Living Tenderly' from *To Mix with Time* by May Swenson to Charles Scribner's Sons; for 'Song: The Railway Train' translated by George Taplin from *The Unwritten Song* edited by Willard R. Trask to the Macmillan Company of New York; for 'Two Paddler's Songs' translated by William Thalbitzer from *The Unwritten Song* edited by Willard R. Trask to the Macmillan Company of New York; for 'A Conversation' from *Under Milkwood* by Dylan Thomas to the Trustees for the copyrights of the late Dylan Thomas, J. M. Dent & Sons Ltd and New Directions Publishing Corporation; for an extract from 'Oliphaunt' from *The Adventures of Tom Bombadil* by J. R. R. Tolkein to George Allen & Unwin Ltd and Houghton Mifflin Company; for 'Dunce Song' from *New and Collected Poems 1924–1963* by Mark van Doren to Hill & Wang Inc.; for 'Angry' by John Donald Williams to the *Daily Mirror* Children's Literary Competition; for 'Between Walls', 'The Thinker' and 'To be Closely Written on a Small Piece of Paper . . .' from *Collected Earlier Poems* by William Carlos Williams to New Directions Publishing Corporation; for 'The Cat and the Moon' by W. B. Yeats to Macmillan & Co. Ltd.

Pictures For the picture facing page 1 to James Hogg; page 3 to Gabriel Barnfield; page 4 to W. Eglon Shaw, the Sutcliffe Gallery; page 7 to Alan Spain; page 9 to Jerry Uelsmann; pages 11, 47 to the Victoria and Albert Museum; page 12 to J. K. St Joseph; pages 16, 72–3 to Harry Callahan; pages 18–19, 80 and title-page to the Trustees of the British Museum; pages 22–3 from *The World of Camera*, photo Yukichi Watabe, to C. J. Bucher Ltd; page 27 to the Philadelphia Museum of Art; pages 30, 39 to the Museum of Modern Art, New York; pages 34–5 to the Alte Pinakothek, West Germany; page 37 to Culver Pictures Inc.; page 48 to Robert Michel; page 51 to Bruce Coleman Ltd; pages 52, 56 to Keystone Press Agency Ltd; page 58 to the West Baffin Eskimo Co-operative; page 60 to Jack Stuler; pages 62–3 to the Borghese Gallery, Rome; page 70 to Peter Blake, Private Collection, London; pages 74–7 from *Ounce, Dice, Trice* by Alastair Reid to Atlantic-Little, Brown & Co.; page 78 from *The Art of Living* by Saul Steinberg to the artist and Hamish Hamilton Ltd.

Every effort has been made to trace owners of copyright material, but in some cases this has not proved possible. The publishers would be glad to hear from any further copyright owners of material reproduced in *Junior Voices*.

List of Illustrations

title-page	Drawing by Hokusai
facing page 1	*Stove*, photograph by James Hogg
page 3	*Freeze*, photograph by Gabriel Barnfield
4	*Old Sea Captain*, photograph by Frank M. Sutcliffe
7	*Trees with Sunlight*, photograph by Alan Spain
9	*On Marriage 1961*, photograph by Jerry Uelsmann
11	*Study of Clouds*, paintings by John Constable
12	*Wytham Wood*, photograph by J. K. St Joseph
16	*Road*, photograph by Harry Callahan
18–19	*Raining Cats, Dogs and Pitchforks*, coloured etching by G. Cruikshank
22–3	*Typhoon*, photograph by Yukichi Watabe
27	*Chilly Observation*, painting by C. S. Raleigh
30	*The Twittering Machine*, painting by Paul Klee
34–5	*The Land of Cockaigne*, painting by Pieter Brueghel the Elder
37	*The Early Pioneers*, anonymous photograph
39	*Baboon and Young*, detail from sculpture by Pablo Picasso
47	*Grasshopper and Plum*, woodcut by Hokusai
48	*Tree Bark*, photograph by Robert Michel
51	*Migrating Ducks*, photograph by Sher Jang Singh
52	*Sea Gull*, photograph by Joseph Scheidt
56	*Tortoise*, photograph by Chris Ware
58	*Muskox Trappers*, coloured lithograph by Pudlo
60	*Light and Water*, photograph by Jack Stuler
62–3	*Apollo and Daphne*, sculpture by Bernini
70	*Girl in a Poppy Field*, painting by Peter Blake
72–3	*Providence 1966*, photograph by Harry Callahan
74	*Words To Be Said on the Move*, drawing by Ben Shahn
75	*Odd Words*, drawing by Ben Shahn
76	*Light Words*, drawing by Ben Shahn
77	*Heavy Words*, drawing by Ben Shahn
78	*The Chair*, drawing by Saul Steinberg
80	*Endpiece*, drawing by Hokusai

Index of Titles and First Lines

A Conversation 5
A funny thing about a Chair 78
A lightning flash 26
A pair of pine roots, old and dark 67
A silver jet 15
A sniffle crouches on the terrace 76
A Tragic Story 38
A trout leaps high 17
A whale! 46
Above my face is a map 10
Angry 33
As I was a-hoeing my lands 59

Beg Parding 49
Between Walls 15
Black as night it cuts through the air 53
Borrowed Armour 17

Cat and the Weather 50
Cat takes a look at the weather 50

Day of Rabblement 42
Daybreak people have been chirping 10
Didn't It Rain 20
Dream Song 10
Duck 51
Dull Day 26
Dunce Song 68

Earwig 57
Eskimo Hunting Song 54

Feel Like a Bird 52
Flit 74
Four Charms 64

Gravel Paths 32
Grey as a mouse 49

Hard by the wildbrooks I met Mary 71
Hey-how for Hallowe'en 64

I am John Jones 31
I am the magical mouse 61
I can hear the trees whispering 32
I feel crinkled when I walk on gravel
   paths 32

I got my poem in perfect order 59
I never had a piece of toast 79
I wanted to use my weapon 54
I was not sleeping when Brother said 32
If I had a wife 68
In a Sailplane 13
In the fall of '16 72
In the house 72
It is in the rock, but not in the stone 1

Living Tenderly 57
Lo the leaves 57

Mean Song 43
Meeting Mary 71
My body a rounded stone 57
My wife's new pink slippers 69

Nora 32
Not even a hat 17
Now, didn't it rain, chillun 20
Now, miller, miller, dustipole 42

O come here! a sunflower! 42
Oliphaunt 49
On a summer's day in the month of
   May 36
On a Sunday 45
On earth there roams a lonely knee 67
On the moon with great ease 29
Once there was a woman went out to
   pick beans 65
One Bright Morning 8
Ooh! 42
Over the dark highway 25

Paddler's Song on Bad Hunting Weather 59
Poem 32
Praise Song of the Wind 21

Rattlesnake 44
Riches 45
Riddles 1
Roads 17

She waddles through the dust 51
Sitting Down, Looking Up 15

Slieve Gua 31
Snickles and podes 43
Social Studies 31
Song : The Railway Train 15
Spring gling 25
Still as a bird 13
Storm Tide on Mejit 24
Sudden Shower 17
Summer Night 26
Suppose the Ceiling went Outside 79

Tching-a-ring-a-ring-tching 43
Teevee 72
the back wings 15
The Ballad of Red Fox 55
The Bee 46
The Big Rock Candy Mountains 36
The Cat and the Moon 28
The cat went here and there 28
The Chair 78
The Cloud-Mobile 10
The cock again 46
The Computer's Spring Greeting 25
The day was dull 26
The ditch in Humber Lane 45
The Feast of Lanterns 43
The Hairy Toe 65
The horny goloch is an awesome beast 57
The Indian of Peru, I think 80
The Kayak Paddler's Joy at the Weather 59
The Knee 67
The Little Man with Wooden Hair 2
The Magical Mouse 61
The Monkey and the Lion 39
The Mouse that Gnawed the Oak-Tree Down 6
The Open-Air Bath 46
The Rook 52

The shopgirls leave their work 45
The Signifying Monkey 39
The Six Badgers 59
The Thinker 69
The Tramp Tree 8
The tree with braces angin out 8
The Two Roots 67
The Whale 46
The wind's spine is broken 24
The World Upside Down 17
There is no place 46
There liv'd a sage in days of yore 38
There was a little man with wooden hair 2
There's-not-a-cobbler-in-the-world 2
To Be Closely Written on a Small Piece of
Paper Which Folded into a Tight Lozenge
Will Fit Any Girl's Locket 6
To change into a hare, say this 65
Transmogrifications 65
Tree Disease 29
Trees with weak roots 21
Twisting turning 17
Two Paddler's Songs 59

We four lads from Liverpool are 43
'What did you say?' 29
What seas did you see 45
What's the matter up there? 33
When I'm out of the house in the open,
  I feel joy 59
Which? 29
Who Said? 2
Woody says, 'Let's *make* our soap 31
Words 74

Yellow sun yellow 55
You feel as if you could jump on them 33
You see the smoke at Kapunda 15

Index of Poets, Translators and Collectors

A. R. Ammons 15

Anthony Barton 8
Bashō 17
Sir Maurice Bowra 54
Gwendolyn Brooks 32
Buson 17, 46

Susan David 32
D. Demetracopoulou 10

James Earp 52

Eleanor Farjeon 71
F. Scott Fitzgerald 72
Melvin Walker la Follette 55

Robert Graves 59

Harold G. Henderson 17, 26, 46
David Hill 26
Patricia Hubbell 32
Ted Hughes 29

Peter Kelso 46
Kikaku 46
James Kirkup 13
Max Knight 67, 79
Augustin Krämer 24

Mei-Lan Law 17
Gary Lewis 25
Vachel Lindsay 6
Lou Lipsitz 25

Walter de la Mare 29
Eve Merriam 43, 72
Christian Morgenstern 67, 79

Mary Neville 31

Onitsura 17, 46

Kenneth Patchen 2, 42, 61
James Payn 79
Anne Pennington 51
Vasko Popa 51

W. Radloff 21
Alastair Reid 74, 75, 76, 77
Charles Reznikoff 45, 80
Theodore Roethke 78, 79

Carl Sandburg 31, 33
Shiki 26
Robin Skelton 45
May Swenson 10, 50, 52, 57

George Taplin 15
William Makepeace Thackeray 38
William Thalbitzer 59
Dylan Thomas 45
J. R. R. Tolkien 49
Willard R. Trask 21, 24

Mark van Doren 68

John Donald Williams 33
William Carlos Williams 6, 15, 69

W. B. Yeats 28